The GRAND
DEMONSTRATION

A Biblical Study of the
So-Called Problem of Evil

JAY ADAMS

The GRAND DEMONSTRATION

A Biblical Study of the
So-Called Problem of Evil

EastGate Publishers
Santa Barbara, CA 93110

New Testament Scripture quotations in this book are from the *Christian Counselor's New Testament*, Jay E. Adams, Baker Book House, Grand Rapids, MI.

THE GRAND DEMONSTRATION

Copyright © 1991 Jay E. Adams
Published by EastGate Publishers
4137 Primavera Road
Santa Barbara, CA 93110

Library of Congress Catalog Card Number 91-73976
ISBN 0-941717-06-2

Printed in the United States of America.

*To Bill—a fellow minister
and valued associate in the work of
the Grand Demonstration.*

TABLE OF CONTENTS

PREFACE

Originally I wrote:

Though I claim no special competence as a prophet, it is with some degree of confidence that I make the following prediction: I predict that the immediate response of a number of readers of this book will be to declare my efforts speculative, dangerous and ill-advised.

Some of these readers will accuse me of going beyond the bounds of propriety, others will attack my credibility as a theologian, while still others will shake their heads in sheer disbelief.

Others, however, will read and understand. They will sigh in relief and (assuming I can find a publisher with courage enough to promote it) may even commend this book as the answer to a question to which they have long sought an answer. Those who agree with what I have written are likely to look upon themselves very differently for having thought about the matters contained in the book and, at the same time, may begin to develop a new appreciation for the greatness and grandure of God. It is for such persons I write.

But, a trusted friend, who read the manuscript, protested, "You're selling your book short." He went on to say (in words to this effect): "You've got something worthwhile here—don't talk it down; sell it in the preface." Well, I believe there is something fresh here that needs to be said, something that has been ignored far too long. And it *is* important. So, I'll put it to you—read it and see if you agree.

Of course, I should like to convince all who read, but I can entertain no such unrealistic hope. Rather, it will be only that less-than-desired number of those who are willing to follow the Scriptures, even when they lead into new and lonely paths, who will respond positively. That is how it is today in Christ's church.

You may wonder at a preface like this, but I say these things to help you realize that I understand the odds against which I am laboring. All I can ask of you then is that, at the outset, you will determine to judge what I have written by the Word of God rather than the opinions of men—including your own. If you do, my sincere hope is that you will be deeply blessed in coming to see the ways of God and men with a new clarity.

INTRODUCTION

"Why did it all happen?" the young man pondered.

He works for the FBI. But at the moment his keen mind was not intent upon discovering the M.O. of some illegal drug dealer. He was focusing on a conversation he recently had with one of America's foremost theologians. The conversation had to do with the M.O. of God!

Following a lecture on the sovereignty of God by the theologian, they had spoken for nearly half an hour. The young man kept pressing his question from several angles. Always, the answers were vague, unsatisfying. This seemed strange to him because he had known of this theologian as one who answered biblical questions straightforwardly.

In his lecture, the theologian declared that God planned all things. That God plans His work and works His plan was the substance of his teaching. So far, so good. But what the young FBI employee wanted to know was why a good God planned evil and, having planned it, why He complains when men sin and consigns those who fail to repent to eternity in hell. These were good questions that deserved better answers than he got.

The theologian's only response was that we cannot know the answer to such questions. We must merely accept what the Bible teaches by faith even when it may be difficult to do so. Human responsibility and God's sovereignty must both be maintained, even though that ends in paradox. He left the young man puzzled and distraught, without a real answer.

A few weeks later this FBI man told me about his conversation and expressed his dissatisfaction. We talked. The discussion was long and spirited. We looked at the Scriptures. We faced the hard truths concerning the so-called problem of evil, the responsibility of man, the nature of God, election, predestination and the free offer of the gospel. When he departed, he was at last satisfied. There was no dodging, no hedging, no retreat into mystery or paradox. Instead, he found resolution.

What happened to change my friend's attitude? He came to understand what I have since come to call THE GRAND DEMONSTRATION. He went away with a new appreciation of the greatness and glory of God.

What we said in that conversation—and more—is what this book is all about. The give-and-take of the original discussion is lost and cannot be reproduced. It did not follow a logical sequence. But, here, in a somewhat more organized form, you have the essence of what was said. It is my hope that you, too, will find resolution in the nothing-less-than stupendous (but sadly neglected) truths of Scripture that are explained in the pages that follow. If you do, for the first time, your outlook on the world will be immeasurably expanded and you will learn, in an entirely new way, to stand in awe of the Almighty God of creation and providence.

1

THE PROBLEM
OF EVIL

The secret things
belong to the Lord our God;
but those things which are revealed
belong to us
and to our children for ever . . .
(Deuteronomy 29:29).

Then the brothers
at once sent Paul and Silas away by night
to Berea. . . .
Now these Jews were more noble
than those in Thessalonica,
and they received the Word
with great eagerness,
examining the Scriptures daily
to see if these things were so.
As a result, many of them believed . . .
(Acts 17: 10-12a).

Is the existence of evil really a *problem*? Is it an unsolvable mystery how evil—and its effects—can exist in a good God's world? Is there no satisfying explanation? No reason so overwhelming that upon hearing it one is compelled to say, "Ah, now I understand"? Can the Christian account for the existence of evil no better than a humanist or atheist? Does God's existence and His revelation of Himself in the Bible throw no light on the question? Must the Christian shuffle his feet and retreat into vague and irrational mouthings when he is pressed on the subject?

For too long answers to these questions given by many theologians have been equivocal, frustrating, and altogether inadequate. If God had not provided a better explanation of His ways and purposes, such answers, of course, would have to suffice. Quoting Deuteronomy 29:29,

> The secret things belong to the Lord our God, but the things that are revealed belong to us and to our children forever,

would be as far as we could go. Speculation about ways of God that He has not revealed to us is wrong. To do it is attempted robbery. If, as He says, unrevealed truths about Himself and His purposes "belong" to Him, and not to us, the attempt to pry those secrets from His hand by means of human reasoning is nothing less than attempted theft. What God has revealed of His nature and ways—and only that—belongs to *us*.

Moreover, to say things about God that He has not first said is to lie about Him and to falsely represent Him as different from what He really is. As Peter says, "When someone speaks, let him speak God's messages" (I Peter 4:11a). But, on the other hand, to *fail* to say all God has revealed in Scripture is to do the same thing. And, that this is precisely the sort of failure of many in regard to the "problem" of evil will become all too apparent as you read on.

Where does this so-called problem of evil emerge? In a good God's world, people want to know how little children can be maimed and killed by drunken drivers, how rape and war and excruciating pain, debilitating disease, torture, and death can occur. Indeed, how can drunkenness, hatred, and deadly germs exist? Does God "reveal" answers to these questions, or are they but "secrets" that "belong" exclusively to God?

To say that all evil is the result of the fall of Adam is perfectly true—but piteously inadequate. That response merely moves the question back a step: how could there be a fall? To suggest that Satan is the cause of the fall, again, is true, but only pushes the inquiry back an additional step: how could the devil exist in a sovereign, good God's world? That is the so-called problem of evil.

The Christian is not left speechless; God *has* revealed Himself concerning this matter. And, He has done so unequivocally, satisfyingly. The problem is not stated properly. It should be put this way: when God has given an unmistakably clear and sufficient reply to such questions, why do theologians persist in saying that He has not? Why do they go through the foot shuffling routine only to hem and haw about a fact that is as plain as the way of salvation itself? The answer, I am afraid, is that they are so heavily loaded with humanism that they are either blinded to the truth, or, understanding it, refuse to teach it out of fear of what others may say.

Christian Scientists attempt to solve the "problem" of evil by denying its existence. There is no such thing as sin, sickness or death, they say. Belief in this triad of evils is but the "error" of "mortal mind." But they implode their own belief by this internally-inconsistent, self-contra-dictory explanation. If there is no such thing as evil, if God is all, and all is God (as they also teach), then, this all-knowing god of which every human being is a part, cannot err, and there is no such thing as erring "mortal mind."

Moreover, there is nothing to correct, no teaching to be given: all, being god, already know all truth—fully. But, as is evident to every person whose thinking has not been hopelessly convoluted by Mary Baker Glover Patterson Eddy's dogmas, the attempts of Christian Science practitioners to "heal" by mind cure that which does not exist, cannot err and needs no further instruction, are not merely fruitless, but the epitome of unmitigated nonsense. These very attempts at correction and cure belie the teaching of the non-existence of evil and its effects. As Mark Twain once quipped, Christian Science is like a snake trying to swallow itself, tail first.

Arminians and Process theologians take a different route around the "problem" of evil. Both, in effect, deny the sovereignty of God. In one way or another, to clear God of the charge of being the Author of sin, they erode His omnipotence and/or omniscience. Either He knew about evil's future existence, when creating the world, and though desiring otherwise was powerless to prohibit it (Arminianism), or He was a God Who didn't know what He was doing when He created the universe (Process Theology). Only since its entrance into creation has He come to know about evil and has, at length, taken emergency measures to counter it. Thus, the death of Christ, rather than the grand climax of history—planned from the foundation of the world—becomes an afterthought.

In either case, that God planned the existence of evil and providentially brought it into human history is emphatically denied.

The kind of wimpish god postulated by these two errant theologies is not the sovereign, all-knowing, all-powerful God of Scripture. Jehovah knows—and "declares"—the end "from the beginning" (Isaiah 46:10). There are no surprises for Him. How could there be since He planned all things from the beginning? The God of the Bible "works all things after the counsel of His own will" (Ephesians 1:11). Nothing, therefore, is impossible for Him to do that He wishes to do. Evil is not some run-away element in the universe, some quirk over which He has no control.

To "save" God from the "charge" that He planned evil's existence, they have emasculated

Him! Think about it: He better have planned evil, because if He did not, the world is out of His control at the most crucial point! Is it worse to think that there is no purpose for evil, no plan, no good end in view? Or that there is?

The Arminian and the Process Theologian have made God subservient to His own creation. He has become a god who reacts rather than One Who sovereignly acts. One who learns from man what he previously did not know. Such a god is no god at all. He is no better than the gods of paganism. He is not the God of Paul.

Over against these views are Reformed thinkers who carefully preserve God's sovereignty by maintaining that He not only always knew all things past, present and future, but has decreed them. Both Arminianism and Process Theology are denied. And, of course, Christian Science's denials of sin, sickness and death are rejected.

So far, so good. But the theologian, lecturing to the audience in which the young FBI agent sat was Reformed. Yet, he, too, failed to answer the crucial question: how can evil exist in a good God's world? Why did God plan evil? What is its purpose? If He hates evil and punishes those who commit sin, how could God ordain it? Here, with him, most Reformed theologians run aground, shuffle feet, and eventually retreat into mystery and paradox.

Is there a better answer? Does Scripture speak more definitively about the matter? Or, must Christians forever, generation after generation, stumble over it? Must they too declare the existence of evil an unsolved (and unsolvable) "problem"?

In the next chapter, I intend to show you that there **is** a solution to the so-called problem of evil. It is a solution that should be grasped and treasured by every Bible-believing Christian. It is an intellectually-satisfying answer, that (I admit) may at first unsettle you. But, most important, it is biblical and therefore belongs to you and your children; it is among those things that God has *revealed*.

In the chapter to follow, I hope to show that the so-called problem of evil is in no sense a *problem* at all (except as proud sinners make it so), but, rather, is basic to the grandest spectacle of all time. Indeed, I hope to show that it is nothing less than an insult to the God of creation to call it a "problem."

In the solution that I shall offer to the so-called problem, lies a great truth about God and about human life that, for too long, has all but lay buried. It is a truth of such significance and wonder that I can call it nothing less than the Grand Demonstration.

2

THE GRAND
DEMONSTRATION

What if God,
wishing to demonstrate His wrath
and to make known His power
endured with great patience
the vases of wrath fitted for destruction,
in order to make known
the riches of His glory
toward the vases of mercy,
that He designed beforehand for glory
(Romans 9:22, 23).

This chapter, though not long, is the heart of the book. If you understand and accept the teaching of Scripture unfolded here, you will see how all that follows is not only consistent with, but flows inevitably from it. And you will have, in your possession, Paul's "solution" to the "problem" of evil.

In order to "solve" the "problem" we must look carefully at a crucial passage of Scripture:

> What if God, wishing to demonstrate His wrath and to make known His power, endured with great patience the vases of wrath fitted for destruction, in order to make known the riches of His glory toward the vases of mercy, that He designed beforehand for glory (Romans 9:22, 23).

These words of Paul grew out of a discussion of God's rejection of Israel, His engrafting of the Gentiles into the church, and how these events accord with the plans and purposes of God. In essence, Paul says, God's actions are not some afterthought, but, rather, the outworking of a grand, overall, eternal plan.

In this section, Paul speaks of the unconditional election of some to eternal life and the wrath of God to be poured out on the non-elect. Paul wrote the words quoted above in the midst of teaching that which people do not like to hear, because it lowers them to their proper place as dependent, created beings and raises God to His rightful place as Creator and Sustainer of all.

This is a declaration about the ways of God with men that deals directly with the so-called problem of evil. What do these words mean? What is Paul saying?

First, let us understand that Paul is dealing with ultimate questions. It is not some secondary issue about which he is commenting. In these words, he pushed the curtain of God's heart back as far as God would allow him. Here, perhaps beyond every other passage of Scripture, you penetrate into the ultimate meaning of the universe.

Here, through the apostle Paul, God tells you the reason why He ordained evil. He unveils the supposed mystery, dissolves the apparent paradox. Paul says that God endures with longsuffering the vases (vessels, pots, jars) that were fitted for destruction *in order to demonstrate and make known* His wrath. Likewise, sin entered the world so that He might make known the enormous wealth of His glory by pouring out His mercy on the vases designed beforehand for eternal life.

In a previous example (Romans 9:17), Paul used the same word, *demonstrate*, and made the very same point. He says God raised up Pharaoh (i.e., brought him onto the scene of world history) in order, by him, to *demonstrate* to all the land (or earth) His divine power (cf. Exodus 9:16: ". . . that I might *display* [or *demonstrate*] my strength in you," *Septuagint*).

It is instructive to note that the verb, used eleven times in the New Testament (exclusively by Paul and the writer of Hebrews), occurs in Romans 9:17 in the middle voice. This form of the verb means "to demonstrate *for myself*," "for my benefit," or "on my own account." Plainly, Paul is saying that divine judgment on Pharaoh and Israel served God's own interests. To know this is important because it shifts the focus from man to God.

Does that surprise you? Trouble you? If so, consider why. How would you expect the Creator of all things to act, if not in His own interests? Do you react negatively when God speaks of

Israel as "the people which I formed for Myself, that they might set forth My praise" (Isaiah 43:21)? If you have trouble with this, it is probably because you have been deeply-dyed in the humanistic dogma that exalts man and dethrones God. One thing every Christian needs to learn is that God acts *in His own interest*.

But, back to Romans 9:20, 21. There is a difference in the verbs used to describe the making of the two sorts of vases. In speaking of the vases of wrath (i.e., those destined to receive God's wrath) that are "fitted" for destruction, Paul uses a word that means "made appropriate to, adapted to." In writing of the vases designed beforehand for glory, he uses a word that means "prepared" or "made ready for." Why the difference; what is its significance?

Vincent Taylor explains most succinctly:

> . . . *fitted for destruction* . . . describes the character of the vessels . . . . To use a similar phrase of the *vessels of mercy* would suggest they are deserving of God's glory.[1]

---

1. Vincent Taylor, *Commentary on Romans*. London: Epworth Press, 1955, p. 66. Taylor, in a Methodist-sponsored commentary, has no reason to show bias toward our interpretation.

Paul, therefore, does not change verbs to weaken the import of the phrase. Quite to the contrary. He says plainly that some were ordained to suffer eternal destruction. His intention is to be sure not to upgrade man too highly; he would not have him think that God's glory is going to be awarded to people because of their character or good works. It depends solely on the grace and mercy of God. *All* deserve destruction; by unbelievable mercy, *some* are rescued from it. Wrath is deserved; glory is not. This is the essence of grace. It is in order to preserve, at all costs, the truth that salvation is the result of grace—and in no way dependent on man's works (or even his foreseen faith)—that he avoids the word that might possibly be misunderstood to teach such a thing.

But, in the discussion, Paul plainly says that God ordained evil and its consequences, upon those who were fitted for it, *so that* ". . . the divine power might have a field of display."[2] Hodge goes so far as to say,

> This is precisely the principle on which all punishment is inflicted. It is that the true character of the divine law-giver should be known. This, of all objects, when God is concerned, is the highest

2. *Ibid.*, p. 64.

and most important . . . On the other hand, the salvation of the righteous is designed to show the riches of his grace.[3]

It is by decreeing evil's existence that both objects could be attained. God's wrath and power directly released against evil men and angels displays a side of His nature that could be known in no other way. Only evil, evil in all its heinousness, could bring it forth. It took the raping of women, war, the mutilation of children to arouse and manifest it. Moreover, the riches of His grace and mercy could not be exhibited apart from the presence of undeserving, helpless, rebellious creatures who cared nothing for the honor of their Creator.

That God chose this speck in the universe as a theatre on which to demonstrate His wrath and power as well as His grace and glory should not surprise us. As when He chose Israel, He made it known that it was not because of their goodness or because they were so great a people, but because He wanted to do a work that would reflect Himself in all that He did (Deuteronomy 7:7, 8); so too, it seems, God chose an inconspicuous planet (that we call Earth) on which to demonstrate His nature. Once again, we see

---

3. Charles Hodge. *Romans*. Philadelphia: Wm. & Alfred Maritien, 1861, pp. 229, 233.

pure, undeserving grace at work.

This fact should humble us. Indeed, if God had placed beings on this earth who, in time, would become sinners on whom He desired *only* to display one side of His nature—His wrath—and had determined not to save any of the rebellious race, He could well have done so, since mankind deserves nothing from God. But He didn't! In a magnanimous act, He demonstrated to all creation that His nature included not only a holy wrath against evil, but a compassionate mercy as well. The effect of this for us is that some undeserving sinners will, by grace, enter into glory.

Let us, then, reject all of those unsatisfying responses that leave us with a "problem" of evil. Instead, let us vigorously affirm that the Spirit, through Paul, has resolved the problem. By the existence of evil and the ways in which He has manifested His nature in responding to it, God has been getting glory to Himself:

> I raised you up, so that [for My benefit] I could demonstrate My power by you, and so that My Name would be proclaimed throughout the whole earth (Romans 9:17).

Pharaoh's case is unique in that he appeared at an important juncture in redemptive history as a conspicuous example of God's wrath and mercy (to Israel). The death and resurrection of Jesus Christ demonstrates even more clearly both the wrath and the grace of God (cf. Ephesians 2:7). And it is now the task of the redeemed people of God to "make known" God's wisdom to all creation (cf. Ephesians 3:9-11). For whom this is done is the concern of the next chapter.

3

WHO IS THE
AUDIENCE?

To me, the very least of all saints,
this grace was given
to announce to the Gentiles
the good news
of the inexhaustible riches of Christ,
and to bring to light
what the arrangement of the secret
that for ages was hidden by God,
the creator of all things,
is like.
This was so that God's
many-sided wisdom
might now be made known by the church
to the rulers
and to the authorities
in the heavenly places
in agreement with the eternal purpose
that He accomplished
through Christ Jesus our Lord
(Ephesians 3:8-11).

When something is displayed, it is displayed *before* someone. A display is of no value if there is no one to view it. When there is a demonstration, it is demonstrated *to* someone. God's Grand Demonstration has been taking place and still continues to take place before hundreds of thousands of intelligent beings throughout the universe. This has been going on ever since the fall of Satan and the angels who "left their proper dwelling place" (Jude 6).

In his sinful self-importance, man thinks and acts as if he were the only creature in the cosmos. He is so impressed with himself that he speaks as if the universe were created for him. However, the Bible makes it abundantly clear that this is not so. The universe was made for God: ". . . all things were created through Him and for Him" (Colossians 1:16b). In the Bible we also read of myriads of angels (Revelation 5:11), living beings (Revelation 4), Cherubim (Psalm 99:1; Ezekiel 11:22), Seraphim (Isaiah 6), Powers (I Peter 3:22), Thrones (Colossians 1:16), Dominions (Colossians 1:16), Authorities (I Peter 3:22), and Principalities (Ephesians 6:12). Though there may be some overlap in these designations of extra-terrestrial beings, it is clear that man is not alone in the universe.

Indeed, some of the angels—Gabriel (Daniel 8:16; Luke 1:19) and Michael (Daniel 12:1; Jude 9; Revelation 12:7)—are even known by name. All angels do not seem to be alike. There are good angels and fallen angels (demons). Some are simply called "angels"; others, "archangels." Occasionally, one is said to be "a strong angel" (Revelation 5:2; 10:1), presumably over against others that are not quite so strong.

What are the angels? They are, as their name means, "messengers" from God, sent on errands to serve Him by ministering to us (Hebrews 1:14). But this name "messenger" is, possibly, a name properly given to them only from a human point of view. Whether they are beings living elsewhere (Jude speaks of some leaving their proper dwelling place) in the galaxies of the universe, who are summoned by God when needed, or simply non-corporal beings that attend Him and do His bidding, we do not know. When they appear to man, they always seem to take male human form. So like man are they, on such occasions, that some "have entertained angels without realizing it" (Hebrews 13:2).

But, one thing we do know for a fact is that angels are interested and involved in the Grand Demonstration of God's Nature that has been taking place on our planet.

Whether other beings from other planets in other solar systems and galaxies are also aware of what is happening here, the Bible does not say. It doesn't say, specifically, that other worlds are inhabited. But it would seem very likely that the angels are but part of a vast throng of intelligent (and possibly sinless) beings who intently view what God is doing here. In Daniel, for instance, there is a group of beings (possibly angels) who are most appropriately called "watchers" (Daniel 4:13, 17, 23). In context, it is apparent that they are acutely aware of what is transpiring here on earth. But, concerning interplanetary theology, I shall say no more; there will be time enough for that when we discover some race of beings on some planet other than ours.

If you understand something of how great the universe is (no one has been able to measure it yet!) and how small our planet is in contrast, you will soon recognize how insignificant you and I, who live on this speck in creation, are. This should not only humble you, but help you to understand better how great a thing it is for us that God should determine to use this planet and the human race to carry out His grand purpose.

Who is His audience? Well, to begin with, the human race itself. In making His power known in the life of Pharoah, He did so in all the earth (Exodus 9:16). And, of course, there are the angels who are so intimately involved and interested in this world. What other creatures are watching and how many there are, we do not know. But, from indications in the Scriptures it is certain large numbers of the "heavenly host" are privy to what is going on.

Surely, for such an auspicious demonstration, there is a great audience attuned, possibly the entire universe. If anything, then, just thinking about the fact that God is "making known" His power and wrath, and His mercy, grace and glory through you, as a member of the race He has chosen in which to do so, should humble you. What a grand scale it is, on which this drama—the greatest of all time—is being portrayed! Think of it. And it is a drama in which you are playing a part!

Consider, once more, the angels. It is they, from the Bible, about which we know the most. At Jesus' birth, angels actively participated in revealing God's purposes to Mary, Joseph and the shepherds. At His temptation, angels ministered to Christ. At His death and resurrection, they appeared on various occasions, and, before them, He ascended to the heavenly throne from which, at the second coming, He will descend in the company of a multitude of them (II Thessalonians 1; Jude 14).

The entire demonstration has been of interest to angels from the beginning. The events having to do with the fall and redemption are "things angels desire to look into" (I Peter 1:12). The word Peter used denotes an extreme curiosity such as would be evidenced when one cranes his neck in order to see.

In Christian worship—a place where much of the drama of redemption is carried on—angels are present (I Corinthians 11:10). They care for the saints of God in the exigencies of life (Matthew 18:10; Psalm 91:11). When apostles were abused for preaching the Word, they became a "spectacle" to watching angels (I Corinthians 4:9). When a sinner is converted, angels rejoice in heaven (Luke 15:7), doubtless praising God for the demonstration of His grace. They are constantly coming to and leaving from the earth (John 1:51; Genesis 28:12). Christ's defeat of Satan was a *public* display (Colossians 2:15), and as Savior, preachers "placarded" Him before men and angels (Galatians 3:1).

As viewers of the various stages of the earthly outworking of God's Grand Demonstration of His nature, angels praise God for His mighty works (Revelation 15:3, 4). And it is what God is doing in and by the church that heavenly authorities come to know and understand God's eternal purposes (Ephesians 3:9-11). It is of particular interest that in the song (or early creedal statement) found in I Timothy we read that Christ was "seen of angels" (3:16). And the festal gathering of the church in heaven is attended by angels (Hebrews 12:22, 23).

Much more could be said about the heavenly audience that for centuries has been viewing the manifestation of God's plan on this earth, but perhaps I have said enough to convince you that the existence of evil in the human race does have an important part to play in God's Grand Demonstration of Himself to His creatures (I say nothing of the interest of the angels in what is happening to those angels that sinned).

We can fully agree with Wick Broomall, who wrote:

> If God planned from eternity to save some of Adam's fallen race, how is he absolved from causal agency in Adam's sin? The believer will answer . . . by affirming that God permitted Adam's sin for some wise and holy purpose.[1]

---

1. Wick Broomall, *The Encyclopedia of Christianity*, Vol. 4. Marshalltown: Jay Green, Publishers, 1972, p. 172.

Yes, exactly so! Only the purpose is not unknown (as Broomall's words seem to imply); it is clearly stated: to make His nature manifest. This purpose, for His own reasons, God considers "wise and holy." And, since He is the all-wise and perfectly holy One, we may be sure that His reasons (unknown to us) are sufficient.

Perhaps in demonstrating His wrath toward sinners on earth, God is graciously warning other residents of His universe. In demonstrating His mercy He may be showing benevolence to draw them closer to Himself. Surely, in it all, His justice is being displayed and He is receiving honor and praise for it. Mankind has had the privilege of being chosen as the race of creatures that God created for such purposes. If for no other reason than that it pleases God to exhibit His nature by means of the human race, that reason for the Grand Demonstration would be "wise and holy." Let all who have ears hear—He is demonstrating Himself before you too!

4

IS GOD FAIR?

So then, He shows mercy
to whom He wishes,
and He hardens whom He wishes.
You will say to me then,
"Why does He still blame people;
who can resist His will?"
But who are you, my friend,
to talk back to God?
The thing that is formed
won't say to the one who formed it,
"Why did you make me like this?"
will it?
Or doesn't the potter have the right
to make out of the same lump of clay
one jar as a decorative item
and another jar for everyday use?
(Romans 9:18-21)

"If it was the sovereign, eternal purpose of God to demonstrate all sides of His divine nature to men and angels, and if He further determined to do so on a minuscule planet of His universe, among a race of creatures called man, in such a way that some of them would be damned forever and others would spend eternity in joy and bliss in heaven, is that fair?"

People ask the question in a variety of ways, but what it always comes down to is doubt about the fairness of God. The question is not new. Paul himself alludes to it in the very passage of Scripture that we have been studying:

> You will say to me then, "Why does He still blame people; who can resist His will?" (Romans 9:19).

Paul had heard it many times—probably every time he taught the truths that he was teaching in this chapter. The argument goes, "If God has sovereignly determined that some will spend eternity in hell, that's not fair! After all, if God wills it, nobody is powerful enough to resist His will." How shall we answer?

To begin with, the very fact that Paul indicates that this question will be asked proves that what I am teaching about the matter in this book is the same thing Paul taught. Paul says that whenever this truth is taught people will ask that question.

Has it been entering your mind as you are reading along? Then, take heart, you are on the right track. If you have not already resolved the questions surrounding it, by this point you should probably be thinking such thoughts. It is only in response to the teaching that God has sovereignly ordained some to eternal wrath that the question is asked.

Views of the passage set forth by Arminians, that take the edge off the teaching above, fail to elicit any question of fairness. That is expressly because all such interpretations are, themselves, designed to blunt or ward off the obvious meaning of Paul's words. But, it should be apparent to any clear-thinking Christian who is open to the teaching of the Scriptures, and willing to follow it wherever it leads, that any interpretation of Romans 9 that fails to call forth the protest found in verse 19 is incorrect.

"Well, I can see that," you may reluctantly admit, "but what of the charge itself? Agreeing, as I must, that Paul teaches what you have been setting forth, the question still remains, 'Why does God blame people?' Didn't He make them what they are? Can they help it if they fulfill His will?"

Consider Paul's own answer:

> But who are you, my friend, to talk back to God? The thing that is formed won't say to the one who formed it, "Why did you make me like this?" will it? (Romans 9:20).

Paul's response is in two parts: 1. a *rebuke*, leading to 2. a *reason*. Each is couched as a counter question.

The rebuke, "But who are you, my friend, to talk back to God?" is clear and sharp. It is a stinging protest against human presumption. Paul brings the reader up short, just as he is deciding that the complaint about God's fairness might have some validity, and makes him think twice about objecting to the actions of Almighty God. Paul expects His reader to respond as Job did when God confronted him in a similar way (cf. Job 40:1-5; 42:1-6). To object to God's will is appalling. Much in the same vein is God's two-chapter long rebuke of Job (Job 38, 39), where He asks, "Who are you to presume to question what *God* does?" It is a necessary rebuke; particularly today.

After all, what is fairness? And from where does your sense of fairness come? Fairness is based on a standard of right and wrong. But it is God, Himself, Who has given us that standard.

Apart from His biblically-revealed will there can be no objective, absolute standard of righteousness. All else is subjective. One person's opinion of what is fair, therefore, is as valid as the next. In other words, apart from an objective, divinely-revealed standard, there is no way to distinguish what is fair from that which is not. All of which is to say that God is the Determiner of what is right and wrong and, therefore, what is or is not fair. Therefore, any judgment by a human being that an action of God is unfair is wrong, presumptuous, fluffy-headed and needs to be brought into conformity with the Word of God after the objector has repented of bringing the charge.

The charge that God is unfair, like the decision in the Garden of Eden to follow Satan's counsel in preference to God's command, reveals a spirit of rebellious autonomy in the one who makes it. It issues from the arrogant assumption that man can sit in judgment on God. This spirit is dealt with in James 4:11b. No wonder, then, that Paul aims this flaming arrow of rebuke at all such vaunting pride!

In a day in which humanism has invaded the church, and, indeed, is often taught by it, this rebuke is sorely needed. It is appropriate to the sassy, avant-guarde evangelicals, steeped in sunny Los Angeles Christianity, who make man to be far more than he is. Paul puts them all in their place. He asks in disgust, "Who are you to talk back to God?" And, in reply, he doesn't expect some long, subjective exploration of your inner psyche. He looks for subjection.

Modern Christian, have you been awash in the milieu of the insipid, man-centered radio broadcasts and books flowing from Christian media over the last few years? If so, the chances are you have been taught to think more highly of yourself than you ought to think (cf. Romans 12:3). Have you bought into it? In today's church, selfism is rampant. Paul's rebuke is designed to make you think more soberly, biblically, of your place in the universe and your relationship to Almighty God.

As you think through Paul's first response ("Who are you . . . ?") you will see the futility of questioning God, you will become aware of your sinful pride and arrogance, and you will humbly bow before your Maker, confessing with Job, "I lay my hand upon my mouth. . . . I abhor myself and repent in dust and ashes" (Job 40:4b; 42:6).

Though the rebuke is sharp and clear, in it Paul shows concern for the one addressed; he does not merely write him off. Rather than slapping his face, and going his way, he reasons with him in order to bring him to repentance and true belief. He continues with the second question:

> The thing formed won't say to the one who formed it, "Why did you make me like this?" will it? (Romans 9:20b)

Of course, the only sensible answer is, "Certainly not!" He then prolongs the point he is making by asking a third question that even more tellingly stresses the same fact:

> Or doesn't the potter have the right to make out of the same lump of clay one jar as a decorative item and another jar for everyday use? (Romans 9:21).

Again, there can be but one reasonable answer: "Yes, of course the potter does! It is his clay to do with as he pleases."

All analogies fall through if you push them too far (remember the parable of the unjust judge?). The point of this particular analogy is *not* that man is like clay, an inanimate mass of material (which wrong application makes many turn their back on Paul's argument; cf. New Testament commentator C.H. Dodd). Rather, Paul's analogy stresses the *right* of God, like a potter, to make whatever He wishes of that which is His own, according to His own purposes. God does not have to answer to anyone else for doing so (cf. Job 33:13).

Should God have created all men for no other purpose than to consign them to an eternity in hell (which, of course, He didn't—not because man was so precious and valuable, but because God wanted to display both sides of His divine nature) we would have no recourse. There would be no reason to protest. God can do with that which is His own *as He wishes*.

It is difficult for many to come to the place of accepting this fact. But all Paul is saying, in essence, is that God is God and man is man. Because of the corruption of the sinful natures with which we are born, we come into the world as self-centered creatures who think the world revolves around us. It is not until the Copernican revolution of the new birth demolishes our self-centeredness that we are able to understand our true place as planets, not suns.

When you see that you are dependent, not self-determined, then—and then alone—can you appreciate Who God is and who you are. God is the Creator of all things Who made you for His pleasure; He does not exist to please you. He is not some cosmic vending machine that will give you whatever you want when you insert the proper prayer coins. You were made to glorify Him either as a vessel of mercy or as a vessel of wrath. It is not incumbent upon God to glorify you. That He has chosen to save you, Christian, should not merely please you; it should astonish you.

It is utterly important to learn your proper relationship to the sovereign Creator and Lord of the universe. Only as you see Him as the divine Potter, Who holds absolute rights over the clay to do with it *as He pleases* can you truly look upon the Grand Spectacle with interest, appreciation and profit. Only then can you cry out with the angels:

> You are worthy to receive glory and honor and power because You created all things and by Your will they exist and were created (Revelation 4:11).

The charge of "unfairness" could be sustained only if you deserved something from God that He fails to give. But God owes man nothing whatsoever except the wages of sin—eternal death, hell. All goodness from His hand, showered down upon you is purely out of grace. Even before the fall, mankind had no claims on God.

The race was made by Him, for His use.

The question posed in Chapter One is "How can evil (and its devastating effects) exist in a good God's world?" You now know the answer: evil ultimately serves a good purpose. Its existence makes it possible for God to demonstrate to all the universe what He is like. There are aspects of His nature that could only be brought forth by evil itself. We would never have known the wrath of God apart from the existence of evil. God's justice demands that His wrath be loosed only upon rebellious, unrepentant creatures who deserve it. Nor would we have been able to know the depths of mercy and grace deep within the heart of God that are manifested only in the death of His Son, had not the need of sinners drawn it forth. Humanity, along with the rest of creation, would be immeasurably impoverished in its knowledge of God's nature had not the Grand Demonstration happened. It was evil, then, that made this demonstration possible.

Does this ultimate purpose make evil good? No. Evil is evil; it can never be anything else. It is a horrible, arrogant manifestation of creaturely hubris. Evil is not a substance that can be handled, like butter that is spread on bread. It is a relationship between creature and Creator. It is, in essence, rebellion against one's Maker that has as many manifestations as God has laws that man can break. "Sin," said John "is

51

lawlessness" (I John 3:4). God says do something; you don't—that's sin. He says don't do something; you do—that too is sin. Sin is disobedience to God.

The word *evil*, however, is used also to designate all those ills in this world that we experience as the result of Adam's sin: pain, sickness, sorrow, death. Suffering, due to God's curse, is linked with sin by the Westminster Standards, in the telling phrase "sin and misery." These miseries are in the world not as part of the divine creation; they have come as the result of man's sin. Yet, as a part of God's plan, they too manifest a good God's nature.

In a lesser way than an eternal hell, these temporal judgments demonstrate God's justice and mercy. His justice is seen in His refusal to allow sin to go unpunished; His mercy in the way in which misery restrains men from further sin and greater wrath, and in the way in which it drives the elect to Christ. Evil—considered either as disobedience or as the misery men suffer in consequence of it—is, therefore, in harmony with the Grand Demonstration.

"But is evil according to the will of God? Doesn't God will righteousness?" The answer to that question is the concern of the next chapter.

5

DOES GOD FULFILL HIS WILL?

What if God,
wishing to demonstrate His wrath
and to make known His power,
endured with great patience
the vases of wrath fitted for destruction,
in order to make known
the riches of His glory
toward the vases of mercy,
that He designed beforehand for glory
(Romans 9:22, 23).

"Our Lord and our God,
You are worthy to receive glory
and honor and power
because You created all things
and by Your will
they exist and were created"
(Revelation 4:11).

When Paul's imaginary objector asks, "Who can resist His [God's] will?" he implies an important truth: the will of God is inevitable. God does what He wants. It is muddled thinking to write,

> The sovereignty of God is indeed absolute and his will cannot fail of fulfilment; but to conceive of the divine sovereignty in such a way that nothing whatsoever can happen that is not in accord with the will of God (rather than holding that nothing whatsoever can happen that can defeat the will of God) means, if it is taken to its logical conclusion . . . that even the closing or opening of a door and all the moves in a game of chess are predetermined by God . . . it is difficult to see how such a view does not leave us

with a God who is the author of sin in the world inasmuch as he is regarded as having sanctioned and decreed it for the promotion of his own purposes . . . as the conclusion of his discussion of divine election, the apostle does not pretend to understand, but simply, by exclamation, marvels at the unfathomable riches of God's wisdom and knowledge and the unsearchability of his ways.[1]

Why does Hughes object to the will of God in specifics as "absolute," and allow it in general: "His will cannot fail of fulfilment?" How can it be fulfilled in general, when it has not been decreed in specifics? The general (eg., the crucifixion of Jesus Christ) is but the outworking of the specifics (the betrayal by the "son of perdition," for instance). Herod, Pilate, the Jews, the Gentiles, etc., in all their specific motives and actions did "those things" that God's "hand" and "plan had predestined to happen" (Acts 4:28). The specifics in each individual case meshed to bring about the event that God ordained. Are we to think that only the crucifixion, and not the events that led to it, was preordained? Apparently Peter thought otherwise. Since the end (Christ's death) is the result of the means, and

---

1. Philip E. Hughes. *The True Image*. Grand Rapids: Eerdmans, 1989, p. 153.

cannot be attained apart from them, the only way in which the will of God can be sure not to "fail of fulfilment" is if the means to it are similarly ordained.

God is the One of Whom it is said, "Not a sparrow falls without the Father" (Matthew 10:29), and that He has numbered every hair of your head (Luke 12:7). Those statements indicate that we are dealing with a God of detail. He is great enough to concern Himself with every detail in all of the universe. It is a small God Who bothers only with ends while caring nothing about means. Those details of divine predestination nicely accord with the opening of a door and the moves in a chess game. Why should the death of Christ be preordained, but not the purchase of nails, hammers and other means of bringing it to pass? What, really, does Hughes avoid in making Jesus the Savior of sinners while denying God sovereignty over the means to do so?

Can ends be so detached from means that one can be predestined while the other may not? Hardly. How do you even distinguish the two? What is one event's means is another's end. This is inevitably true in the cause-and-effect world in which we live. Where would Hughes draw the line? Was the long-prophesied betrayal by Judas, who was entitled the "son of perdition" (i.e., the one who was destined for perdition) an end or a means? Hughes' position is untenable.

Hughes further confuses the issue by using emotion-laden terms about God, saying that if He decreed the presence of sin in His world, that would make Him the "author of sin," Who is "responsible" for it. Decreeing the existence of sin makes God neither. God decreed water, dry land, mountains, birds of the air, but God is none of the above. Decreeing sin does not make Him a sinner. He decreed the entire creation, but must be distinguished from it.

Hughes fails on another score. He fails to recognize that the Bible uses the phrase "God's will" in two distinct senses. Sometimes the words mean that which, from all eternity, God has decreed to happen (Romans 9:19b). This has been called God's *decretive* will, and is precisely what we have been discussing. At other times, however, the words *God's will* mean what has been called God's *directive* will. These are His commands by which He directs men about how they should live (eg., Psalm 40:8).

The matter of two perspectives emerges frequently in the study of the Bible. For instance, we read, "God is not a man that He should repent" (I Samuel 15:29), and yet we also read of God Himself saying, "I repent that I have made man" (Genesis 6:7b). The former verse explains something of the nature of God (He never changes His mind). The latter tells us in anthropomorphic (human) terms what He thinks of man's sinful behavior ("Were I a human being, I'd change my mind about having created man"). To express His displeasure at man's disobedience, He resorts to terminology we can understand (as He does when He speaks of His "hand" or "arm").

To speak of the directive will of God in human terms means that the writer is saying, "This is what God wants (wills) *you* to do." To speak of the decretive will of God means that the writer is telling us what *God* will do. One perspective has man in view as the actor; the other, God.

Now, back to those emotion-laden terms. Is God the "author" of sin because He decreed it? No. Because He has decreed the existence of sin in such a way that men themselves freely (i.e., uncoerced and in accord with their own natures) become the authors of their sin. All depends on how you use the word author.

In his book, *Author, Author*, P.G. Wodehouse occasionally mentions the fact that he used a plot that Bill Townend, with whom he shared ideas throughout life, gave him. Did that make Townend the author of Wodehouse's book? Not at all. But, again, all analogies fail. Wodehouse merely borrowed the plot, doing with it as he pleased, whereas (as we have seen) men work out, specifically, in detail, all that God decrees.

59

But, they do so, in such a way that they are the authors of their own sin. They live their lives; God does not live their lives for them. The story of their rebellion appears *in their own handwriting*. We generally use the word *author* to designate the one who performs the task, the one who sits down at the word processor and hammers out his story. Clearly, it is man, not God, who does that; he, not God, sins.

Which leads us to that other term, *responsible*. Hughes thinks that if God predestined all men's actions, He would be responsible for their sin. But God is not responsible for what men do. They are. That is the kind of people that God created: persons who would be responsible for their actions.

And, you may be sure that God holds men responsible for the lives they lead. Nothing is plainer on the pages of Scripture. To whom could God be held responsible? The thought is absurd. There is no one but Himself to whom God must answer, which means that He answers to no one. To be responsible to one's self totally defeats the concept of accountability inherent in the word. There is no one who can call God on the carpet. He does as He pleases, and He is pleased with what He does. What He does is holy and wise. No one has the right (or ability) to question any of His ways—particularly, weak, sinful, limited and mind-distorted creatures like us. Surely,

God is not responsible to us!

What Hughes fears is precisely what Paul affirms: that God decreed sin "for the promotion of his own purposes." But it is only by conveniently ignoring Romans 9:22, 23 that he can do so. In those two verses, as we have seen, God expressly declares what Hughes denies. God decreed sin in order to demonstrate His power and wrath as well as the riches of His glorious grace.

Again, Hughes uses a question-begging epithet, "sanctions," in speaking of God. His notion is that what God decrees, He sanctions. Therefore, if He decrees evil, He sanctions it. Such language, once more, misses the point. If by *sanctions* Hughes means that God could be said to *approve* of sin, rather than abhor it, clearly, that could not be; everywhere the Bible says the opposite. If, however, what is meant is, while hating sinful rebellion, God, nevertheless, decreed it and bore with it (as Paul says), for holy and wise purposes (Romans 9:22), then that is exactly what God did. But, remember, what God decreed takes place through responsible agents, who, without coercion, do only that which they want to do.

God is neither the author of sin, nor sanctions it (approves of it). He is not responsible for sin, though He decreed it. Those guilty of sinning are responsible. He decrees not merely the ends, but also the means, in this case that sin would be brought into the world by free agents who would be wholly responsible for it.

Consider the following questions Hughes does not deal with :

1. Could man have sinned had not God given him a nature capable of sinning? If not, why did He give him the nature He did?

2. Could man have sinned if God had not sustained him in doing so?

3. If God knew infallibly all that would ever happen—every move of every chess game, every rape and case of child abuse—before He created the world, were not those things certain? If so, and there were as yet no creatures—only God—who made these things certain?

4. If God does not in some sense will the existence of evil deeds, how do they happen? Is God, who (according to Hughes) in no sense wills sin, impotent before evil? If not, how does evil prevail in spite of the almighty will of God?

5. Can God only overrule evil, as Hughes seems to suppose? If so, then what of

Ephesians 1:11? There, Paul certainly tells us that God brings *all things* to pass according to the counsel of His own will—not some merely in response to the will of man.

It is true, as Hughes says, that Paul does not "pretend" to understand the purposes of God with reference to the existence of evil. He does not need to pretend. He *does* understand and wants you to do so too. That is why his words in Romans 9:22, 23, which disclose that purpose, are so clear. To reject such a plain explanation can be due only to such strong prejudice against the truth that it is viewed only with blinders, well-positioned.

But, throughout this chapter one issue has arisen again and again: the matter of the freedom of man. Is man free? In Chapter Six I shall consider that matter.

6

IS MAN FREE?

*Those who walk
according to the flesh
set their minds on fleshly things,
but those who walk
according to the Spirit
set their minds on spiritual things.
Now to have a fleshly mind is death,
but to have a spiritual mind
is life and peace,
because the fleshly mind
leads to hostility toward God,
since it doesn't subject itself
to God's law; nor can it.
And those who are in the flesh
can't please God
(Romans 8:5-8).*

The doctrines of divine sovereignty—embracing predestination, election, etc.—are frequently dismissed as foolish and dangerous teachings that, if accepted and believed, would destroy evangelism, human initiative and responsibility. Only if man is free, we are told, can these important elements of the Christian life be preserved. And if man is free, then, all that has been said so far in this book is untrue and must be rejected. That is the claim of many. Is there any substance to it?

People who confuse predestination and fatalism often say such things. They say, "If I am predestined to be saved, what difference does it make how I live or whether I believe or not? If I'm to be saved, I will be—regardless." That is Muslim fatalism, not predestination. Truly converted persons don't talk that way. They want to live for Christ out of gratitude and by the encouragement of the Word and the Spirit at work in their lives.

Fatalists, I say, talk like that. Fatalists say, "If I'm going to be hit by a truck on the corner of Fifth and Main on July 5, 1992, it will happen—no matter what I do." *Que sera sera.* But, in stark contrast, predestinarians say, "If I'm going to be hit by a truck on the corner of Fifth and Main, on July 5, 1992, it will happen—*because* of what I do." It will be because you were watching that attractive blonde rather than the traffic.

Fatalists say "in spite of"; predestinarians say "because of." The former view destroys responsibility; the latter establishes it. The former makes of man an automaton; the latter a responsible, moral agent. God works through the latter to effect the counsels of His will, not through the former.

Man is not a robot. Neither is he a pawn to be moved about at will in some cosmic chess game. He is a responsible agent, who makes decisions and choices. The divine plan neither preempts responsible human action nor collides with it. God does not have to "overrule" what man does in order to bring about His purposes (as Hughes supposes); rather, He works out these purposes by means of human beings who are ordained to freely choose and decide in a responsible manner. The Grand Demonstration is nothing, if it does not involve human responsibility.

God's predestination establishes human agency; that is a part of His plan. He determined to work through responsible, free agents; not through pawns. God planned not only the ends He desired, but, also, the means by which they would be accomplished. And man, freely, accountably, choosing as he will, is the principal means.

"But how free is man if his life in its entirety is predestined?" you ask.

He is as free as God!

"What?"

Yes, God is free only to act according to His nature, which, of course, is perfect freedom. God *cannot* lie (Titus 1:2); He *cannot* go back on His Word (Romans 11:29). To do so would be out of accord with His nature. Therefore, He would never want to. His holy nature insures His truthfulness and faithfulness. He is limited only by what He is. Unregenerate man, for instance, "cannot please God" (Romans 8:8) because to do so would be contrary to his nature. But, he doesn't want to either. While he cannot know the things of the Spirit of God (I Corinthians 2:11, 12), the regenerate, whose nature has been changed and who has the Spirit dwelling within can (v. 12). He has the mind of Christ (v. 16).

69

Freedom is not the freedom to be something you are not or to become something you cannot. That notion of freedom, all too prevalent, is nonsense! Yet, those who complain about predestination seem to want precisely that. Indeed, all too often, it seems, they have an attitude similar to that which led to the downfall of Adam and Eve. They desire a freedom from God that amounts to autonomy. That, of course, is not possible. Man's nature is such that he is a dependent creature. He depends on the earth and the sun, and on other beings for food, drink and shelter. His life is a veritable web of dependencies and interdependencies. And, whether he will acknowledge it or not, he depends utterly on God—even for his next breath (cf. Acts 17:28; Colossians 1:17).

So, I say again, man is free because he is free to act according to his own nature. But that nature is not self-determined. He acquired the basic stuff of his nature by birth—with all its potentialities and limitations. He was born in a certain century and place with all of the same. Ultimately, if you think it through, it goes back to creation; his nature was acquired through a series of births from God.

But man could never be freer. Surely, he cannot act according to some nature other than his own. Nor can he get out of his own skin. So, the freedom he has is his; which is perfect freedom. But it is not freedom from God or from his God-given nature.

"But, if all is planned, I still don't see how a person can be said to make free, responsible choices."

First, let's establish one thing. You don't feel coerced into making choices or decisions, do you? Don't you consider them your own? And you do bear the responsibility for your choices—don't you? Then, whether you ever fully understand the reasoning behind what I am saying or not, hold on to those facts. Don't allow anyone's intellectualizing to confuse you.

Secondly, man does make choices for which God holds him responsible, because that is the sort of being God made him to be. He is held accountable for his decisions, attitudes and actions because he freely thinks, feels and acts according to his nature. He is himself, not something someone outside pressures him into becoming. God coerces him to do nothing; that is not how God works. God forces no one to sin. Man sins because he wants to, because it is his nature to do so. Therefore, God holds him responsible for his sin.

And, it is not apart from, but through responsible thinking and acting beings that He carries out His plan. It is something like the way in which much of the Bible was written. The Spirit of God was at work in the human writer so as to use his personality and nature to pen what

He wanted, but in no way coercing the writer to do so. The product was a Book that at once was man's and God's. The product of a human life, in a somewhat similar way, is the result of free human agency and divine planning. There are differences, of course; but perhaps, seeing the similarities will help.

A study of Acts 2:22-24; 4:25-28; and 13:26-30, in which human responsibility and the responsible actions of man are intimately juxtaposed to predestination, may also help.

"Much that you say seems to clarify the issue, but somehow, I'm still confused."

Let's put it another way. You are shopping for a car. There are lots of choices. In the end, you choose an American over a Japanese model, though both were in the same price bracket. Now, did you feel compelled to make that decision—or was it your own?

"Well, naturally, it was my decision. No outside force was exerted upon me to make me buy American. I chose to do so."

O.K. Good! Then we can freely say that you freely made that decision, can't we?

"Fair enough."

But now, let me ask you, what is this *you* that did so? Wasn't it a person with a nature that, at a certain point in time, as the culmination of many experiences and acts, would make that—and only that—decision? To say it another

way, it was *you*, the *you* that you were born with
plus what you have done with it over many life-
events that *from within* compelled you to so
decide? You were self-compelled. You acted
according to your nature; given what it was at a
certain time and place in your history. Given a
certain set of circumstances, the you that you
are did what you will do. But, that is freedom, as
full and rich as anyone can have. Yet, the choice
you made was inevitable. Is that much clear?

"Yes."

And was it a responsible decision that you
made?

"Certainly."

When the doors fell off and the motor froze
at 40,000 miles, you had no one to blame for your
poor choice but yourself; you chose American.

"Yes!"

The consequences of our choices follow us.
That is the sort of world God made, and that is
how He works through providence. So, if a choice
is made against Christ—freely made—according
to a person's nature, he too has no one to blame
but himself for the consequences of his fatal decision?

"Well, I guess so. At least I can't see how it
could be otherwise."

No, it can't. And it was only the inner person that he is that compelled him to so choose; no one from the outside was forcing him to do anything. God gave us our natures, natures that would act freely, accountably, in furthering His purposes. Because they are such, we feel no compulsion, coercion, or force. We choose freely according to our natures *and thus fulfill His will.* There is no other way to view the matter: every person is free to be himself; how could he be anything else?

Perhaps it would be wise to conclude this chapter with a summary of the matter by John Calvin:

> . . . the perdition of sinners depends upon the divine predestination of sinners in such a manner that the cause and matter of it are found in themselves (*Institutes*, III:23:8).

7

ELECTION
AND YOU

Blessed be the God and Father
of our Lord Jesus Christ,
Who has blessed us
with every kind of spiritual blessing
in the heavenly places
in Christ,
even as He chose us in Him
before the foundation of the world
to be holy and blameless before Him.
In love He predestined us for adoption
as His own sons through Jesus Christ
in keeping with the good pleasure
of His intention,
leading to the praise
of His glorious grace,
which He presented to us
as a gift in the beloved One
(Ephesians 1:3-6).

That God elected some to eternal life is the astounding fact of the Grand Demonstration. And if you are among the elect, it is that aspect with which you should principally be concerned. I assume that most of those who read this book will be among the elect number of individuals who have been regenerated by the Spirit and have been given the gift of faith. Assuming this, let me address you as such, trying to help you apply what you have learned so far in a practical way to daily living. You have seen that it is true that:

> Jehovah has made known His salvation;
> He has openly shown His righteousness
> in the sight of the nations [Gentiles] . . . .
> All the ends of the earth have seen the
> salvation of our God (Psalm 98:2, 3b).

What should all of this mean to you? Well, I have already mentioned the fact that God has chosen you to be a part of the great drama. That fact alone is overwhelming—if you think seriously about it. But there are four things in particular that I wish to emphasize. The list, however, is by no means exhaustive.

Learning about your part in the Grand Demonstration:

1. *Should humble you.*

When you understand the magnitude of what God is doing on this planet, the fact that creation, fall, and redemption have, as their ultimate object, to reveal the nature of God to man and to the universe, and that He has chosen you to play a positive role in displaying the riches of His glory, how can you not be humbled (not to say floored) by the significance of it all?

You—a puny, worthless rebel—have been chosen (purely by grace) to be one of those in whom God is demonstrating to the universe the goodness, compassion, kindness and grace that lie in the depth of His being! Your salvation astonished angels; shouldn't it have a similar effect on you? It certainly humbled Paul. In speaking of how God demonstrated His grace in his life before men and heavenly beings, he wrote:

To me, the very least of all saints this grace was given to announce to the Gentiles the good news of the inexhaustible riches of Christ . . . so that God's many-sided wisdom now may be made known by the church to the rulers and to the authorities in heavenly places in agreement with the eternal purpose that He accomplished by Christ Jesus our Lord (Ephesians 3:8, 10, 11).

Can you do any less than fall down on your face before Him in praise, gratitude and thanksgiving? What astonishing grace is yours!

2. *Should thrill you.*

Playing a part in a theatrical production is exciting. Participating in the joys of a winning team is exhilarating. But what greater thrill could you have, as a sinful, hell-deserving human being, than not only to have your sins forgiven, washed away in the blood of Christ, but to be chosen by the Lord of glory to receive glory and honor (Romans 9:23) which God has prepared for you from all eternity. It is glorious to triumph in sports or war. But never has this world even conceived of the *riches* of glory that the elect will receive, when in glorifying Christ (II Thessalonians 1:9, 10) they will bask in His glory.

The thrill of cheering on a winning team, of having sided with the victors, and now entering vicariously into the joys of triumph is only the faintest possible example of what you will experience as you participate in the glory and honor of that day when He comes as the glorious, conquering Lord of glory. That is what Peter, who had seen something of the glory of Christ on the mount of transfiguration, meant when he wrote of the future glory of which you will become a partaker at Christ's "revelation" (I Peter 4:13) and of the Spirit of glory that already "rests" upon you (v. 14). Doubtless, that Spirit cannot help but cause joy and a sense of glory in you as He illumines your mind to understand the purpose of God's electing grace and the role He has given you to play in demonstrating it.

3. *Should motivate you.*

If the great, biblical truth set forth in this book has given you new insight into the ways of God and man, surely that knowledge should motivate you to study the Scriptures afresh, looking for specific instances of the Grand Demonstration as the theme, like a rock, thrusts itself upward, surfacing again and again on the pages of Scripture. Soon you will come to view all Scripture differently. These outcroppings of dynamic, basic truth, once perceived, should cast new light on all your study of the Scriptures. Once understood, nothing remains the same. The whole is now cast in the light of the Grand Demonstration, by which God has determined to display His mighty power and the riches of His grace.

4. *Should provide a new interpretation of history and current events.*

Tomorrow's newscast, as well as the pages of history past, should alike provide fresh examples of God manifesting both His power and His grace. Hitler's downfall and the destruction of the Axis powers must be seen as one instance of the justice and wrath of God, poured out in restraint (it is true), but providing a sample and foretaste of "the wrath to come." The Grand Demonstration, which reaches its climax at the General Judgment, will dwarf all previous events by its awesome power and devastation. Yet, now, such current events do provide something of a foretaste by which we may, in part, understand what lies ahead and something of the full revelation of God's nature that is yet to come. The inundation of the world by the flood, the devastation of Sodom and Gomorrah by fire and sulphur, and the destruction of Jerusalem are all held out by biblical teachers as instances that prefigure the coming wrath of God.

From these examples, and others like them, God expects you, day-by-day, to remember that what is really happening all around you is but a meagre part (but, nonetheless a part) of the Grand Demonstration of His nature that will culminate in the denouement known to us as the Second Coming of Christ.

What is true of events foreshadowing the final wrath of God is true also of the glory of Christ. Peter, along with James and John (cf. II Peter 1:16; I John 1:2), in a temporary and fleeting way, experienced the actual glory of Christ. They never forgot it. In this life, you will not do that. But, through their writings, you can read about it and vicariously enter into their experience. Moreover, by a spectacular sunset over the Pacific, in the most minuscule manner, you are experiencing something like the glory to come.

But, more to the point. When something in history or current events goes right, when someone falsely accused of a crime is freed, when a soul is saved, when a prayer is answered, when you read of the triumphs of Augustine, Luther or Calvin over sin and oppression, you learn something of the triumphant glory of Christ's coming victory.

All-in-all, the fact of your election to eternal life, coupled with your new understanding of its purpose and place in the predestined plan of

God, should have a deep, abiding impact on your life, leading to a new devotion to and enjoyment of your faith. How can it be business as usual for you, when you hold a leading part in the Grand Demonstration?

8

THE GOSPEL OF
THE GRAND
DEMONSTRATION

But don't forget this one fact,
dear friends,
that one day with the Lord
is like a thousand years,
and a thousand years
are like one day.
The Lord is not delaying His promise
in the sense that some think of delay,
but He is patiently waiting for you,
not wanting any of you to be destroyed,
but every one
to come to repentance
(II Peter 3:8-9).

So then, as the Holy Spirit says,
"Today, if you hear His voice,
don't harden your hearts . . ."
(Hebrews 3:7-8a).

In the previous chapter I assumed you are one of the elect, that is, one of those whom God from all eternity foreordained to eternal life. As such, your life history will be among those who make known the riches of God's glory.

It may be, however, in the story of your life, though elect, you have not yet come to faith in Jesus Christ, therein experiencing the forgiveness of your sins and entering into the assurance, joys and trials of salvation. If so, perhaps God has planned from all eternity to use this simple chapter to bring you into faith and forgiveness.

God tells us that the reason why He has delayed the second coming of Christ and the final wrap-up of human history for so long is not because of any "slackness" on His part in "fulfilling His promises" (II Peter 3:8, 9), but out of concern for His elect. He is not willing for any of them to perish, but wants all of them to come to repentance (v. 9). That means He has been waiting for *you*.

God's Grand Demonstration will move ahead in stride, never slackening in pace. But it will run only according to the divine time and purpose. God is in no hurry; He brings about all things in their season. Yet, He bids you not to wait, but to come to Christ *now*. He urges you to wait no longer:

> Today, if you hear His voice, don't harden your hearts (Hebrews 3:7, 8, 15).

If you hear this urgent call of God from His Word and know within that you want to enter into the company of God's elect who have professed saving faith in Christ, let me tell you what to do. First, you must acknowledge that, like all other persons born into this world by natural generation, you were born a sinner (Psalm 51:5; Romans 5:12ff). This corrupted and condemned you before God. Moreover, you manifested that sinful nature in many acts of personal sin. As a result, you are both corrupt and guilty before God. Apart from His electing grace in Christ, there is nothing you can do to alter the situation. At this moment, the wrath of God hangs over you like a divine thunderhead.

Ceremonies, good works, rituals, church membership—none of these can wash away your sin.

But, if the Holy Spirit has given you life, resurrecting you from spiritual death, you now desire forgiveness for your sin and rebellion against God. The second thing, therefore, that you must do, in humble reliance on the grace of God alone, in repentance, confessing all your sins and iniquities before a holy God, is to trust in the good news. What is the gospel (i.e., "good news")? Simply this: that Jesus Christ died on the cross for elect sinners, taking the punishment they deserved for all their sins. On that cross, He bore the penalty due them. He was their substitute, the One Who took their place and experienced the wrath of God they deserved. And, to show that God accepted His death as a full and sufficient sacrifice for sin, He raised Jesus from the dead. That is the good news (cf. I Corinthians 15:1-4).

Believe that good news—that Christ died for you, rose from the dead, and will save you from the wrath of God the moment you do. Your sins will be fully and freely forgiven and you can not only know that you are destined for eternal life, but you can begin experiencing something of it right now, here in this life.

Then, having believed and been saved, you should unite with a Bible-believing church in which you can grow under the preaching of the

Scriptures and in the fellowship of God's people. Here, too, you can develop and use the gifts Christ gave you for the building up of His church. Don't put this off; it is essential.

Will you believe? Remember, God holds you responsible for your decision. He expects you to exercise your free agency. You must believe to be saved. He, therefore, calls on you to trust (depend upon) the all-sufficient work of Christ on the cross. Believe now—and be saved!

Today is the day of salvation, while God waits for all the elect to come home. Join the vast throng of those whose robes have been washed in the blood of Christ, and as the galleries of angels and other creatures watch in awe and great joy, demonstrate once again the goodness, grace, and glory of God!

9

OF MEN
AND ANGELS

It was concerning
this salvation that the prophets
who prophesied about the grace
that would be yours
searched and sought,
trying to find out to what
or what period
the Spirit of Christ in them pointed
when He testified beforehand
about the sufferings of Christ
and the glories that would follow them.
To them it was revealed
that they were serving not themselves
but you in these things
that now have been declared to you
through those who,
by the Holy Spirit sent from heaven,
announced the good news to you,
things that the angels
desire to look into
(I Peter 1:10-12).

When Protagoras, the father of sophistry, wrote, "Man is the measure of all things," he struck a note that is discordant with that which is sounded forth in the Bible. Not the will of man, but the will of God is the standard for faith and life, say all the writers of Scripture. All the world is divided between these two viewpoints. On the one hand are the humanists, present sons of the leaders of the so-called enlightenment who, in turn, were the children of the Greek philosophers. This whole line of thinking stressed the supposed autonomy of man. Actually, the basic principle underlying it was first expressed in the Garden of Eden by the old serpent, the father (originator) of lies, when he seduced Eve into thinking that man, not God, should determine what is right and wrong.

From the outset of human history he has endeavored by every sort of stratagem to persuade mankind of the hypothesis, possibly first formulated as a principle by Protagoras in the words cited above. But it is a lie; man is not the measure of all things.

Even the Athenians were wise enough to see this and expelled Protagoras from the city and burned all his works.[1]

As far as we know, evil began with Satan and the angels who "left their proper habitation" (Jude 6). What sort of event this reference describes, we do not know. But in itself it reveals the same spirit, of wanting what one is not entitled to, that was present in the Garden, in the philosophy of Protagoras, in the "enlightenment," and in modern humanism. In all, there is an attempt to assume for one's self rights and privileges that God has retained for Himself.

It is conceivable that there could have been rebellion by other creatures before the devil's fall. But we know nothing of it; and it seems very unlikely. What we do know of the fall of the devil and his angels is itself scanty enough. Because of this, some have thought that two biblical references, one in Isaiah and the other in Ezekiel,

---

1. R.D. Hicks, trans. *Diogenes Laertius*, II. The Loeb Classical Library. New York: G.P. Putnam's Sons, 1925, p. 456.

refer to the satanic revolt.

The two passages, Isaiah 14:12-17 and Ezekiel 28:1-17, have to do with the fall of two kings, as both passages clearly say, who (again, in the same spirit of sinful autonomy) sought to exalt themselves above God. The passages refer to the downfall of the kings of Babylon and Tyre. The grandiose terminology used throws some off track; but it is merely Hebrew hyperbole showing how self-important these kings had become. They thought of themselves in the light described. Not only are the kings named, as such, but they are explicitly called "men" (Isaiah 14:16; Ezekiel 28:1, 2). Nowhere are they called angels.

All, then, that we know of the angels or of sin before Adam's is found in scattered references, none of which provide adequate information to paint a complete picture of the angelic rebellion. What we *can* say, however, is that from all we read angelic rebellion seems no different from human rebellion in essence. That is why some could so easily identify Satan with the descriptions of the two kings who exalted themselves above God. If we were to take Protagoras' principle and apply it to the angels who sinned, we would write, "Angel is the measure of all things."

Why God chose to redeem men and not angels is also unknown. Possibly, it is because

95

the rebellion of the angels was pristine and not in response to the lies and temptations of another. But that is mere speculation. What is certain is that, as the writer of Hebrews observes, Jesus Christ chose not to become an angel, but a man. And, even though it seems that angels were originally of a higher order of beings than man, now, because of the incarnation and the glorification of humanity in Christ, mankind has been raised far above all other creatures (I Peter 3:21, 22; Psalm 8:5, 6). There is now seated in the heavenlies, on the throne at the Father's right hand, a God-*man*, Christ Jesus! The enormity of this exaltation in Christ, again dramatically demonstrates the greatness of the divine glory, described by Paul as "the riches of His glory" (Romans 9:23).

One might expect God to redeem angels, beings of a race superior to our own, so superior that, even in their state of condemnation, command respect (Jude 8-10). Angels seem to have been (and the elect among them seem still to be) in the immediate presence of God. Yet, the fact that they were by-passed in favor of a puny, insignificant race of laughably rebellious men (Psalm 2:4), floating in space on a very minor planet under a curse, makes the grace of God all the more striking. It was not mighty angels, but weak men He stooped to redeem. How infinite that demonstration proved to be! How magnificent it proved His goodness and mercy to be!

Now, as a result, men—created lower than the angels—have become the recipients of angelic ministry (Hebrews 1:14). And, some day when Christ returns, it is not angels who will judge men, but men who will judge angels (I Corinthians 6:3)!

Indeed, in the New Testament angels become almost a foil against which the drama of redemption takes place. God's dealings with angels, by comparison and contrast, serve to enlarge His mercy and grace toward man.

Indeed, it seems strange that angels, who appear from time to time to deliver information to men and who seem privy to far more heavenly truth than we, should so seek to learn more about God's Grand Demonstration that they "crook" their necks to peer into the prophetic facts about salvation (I Peter 1:12b). It would seem necessary, then, for the Grand Demonstration to take place to complete the education of angels (and other creatures). Apart from evil and all the outworkings of redemption in relation to it, it would appear that they could never have learned of God's compassion on creatures that had sinned. A part of His nature would have gone unrevealed. Their knowledge is incomplete, but growing. Like the prophets, they delivered messages they only partially understood (cf. I Peter 1: 11).

97

All-in-all, what is said of angels enhances and intensifies the Grand Demonstration that is taking place on earth.

The observing function of angels is prominent. Not only may it be found in I Peter 1:12 and in the rejoicing of the angels over repentant sinners (Luke 15), but also in an interesting passage in Luke 12:8, 9 where one who confesses Christ as Lord (or refuses to) *before men*, will find that Jesus will confess or deny him *before the angels of God* (i.e., before the angels who did not sin). To confess or deny *in the presence of the angels* is to do so in the ultimate outworking of the Grand Demonstration at the judgment as the angels who accompany the Lord Jesus witness His acknowledging (or refusal to acknowledge) them (cf. Matthew 25:31).

Angels, no less than man, are a part of the grand plan of God. The fall of Satan and "his angels" (i.e., those who followed him) no less than the fall of man was predetermined. But, in the case of angels, it seems that they did not fall *as a race* the way mankind did. There were some—probably the vast majority (God speaks of innumerable hosts of good angels)—who never fell at all and who remain faithful to God to this day. These are called the "elect" angels before whom, incidentally, important transactions of Christ's church take place (I Timothy 5:21). But these angels were elected not from among the masses of apostate angels to be redeemed, but simply from the entire number of angels to be created as those who were destined never to fall. Again, this stresses the fact that divine election is not based on works or anything in the creature himself. Rather, it is a function of the grace of God, planned from eternity to facilitate the outworking of the Grand Demonstration.

Ordinarily, we do not tend to think much of angels and the rest of the universe. That, of course, is because of our sinful man-centeredness. We are all born Protagorians. Humanism is a curse that blinds us to many of the realities around us. One of the most important is the reality of the unseen world. True, we know relatively little about it, but in the Scriptures there is quite a bit more said than at first meets the eye. In particular, much is said about angels and their activities and relations to men. There is not so much about other creatures that appear to be less directly related to us. (In Acts 23:8ff, for instance, angels seem distinguished from pure spirits.) It would be useful sometime for you to do a Bible study (using a concordance and good Bible dictionary) of what God says about angels. You may be surprised at the wealth of Scriptural material.

It might also be of value to read Frank Peretti's two volumes, *This Present Darkness* and *Piercing the Darkness* to gain a vivid sense of the reality of the unseen world. Peretti is a good writer, who does much to make the other world and its impact on ours come to life. Unfortunately, the books are frequently unsound doctrinally. Be careful about Peretti's ideas of "prayer cover," wings of angels, direct revelation, and direct influence (rather than indirect solely through temptation) on human beings. These are serious defects in his works. But, in spite of these defects about which I must warn you, in this earth-centered society in which we live, on balance, there is still something of a sense of the other world to be gained from reading Peretti. But read with discernment!

10

THE RICHES
OF HIS GLORY

And all of us,
with unveiled faces,
seeing the glory of the Lord
as if it were reflected in a mirror,
are being transformed
into His likeness
from glory to glory,
as from the Lord the Spirit
(II Corinthians 3:18).

This temporary light affliction
is producing for us
an eternal weight of glory
that is beyond all comparison,
since we aren't looking
for the things that are seen,
but rather
for the things that are unseen.
The things that are seen
are temporary,
but the things that are unseen
are eternal
(II Corinthians 4:17-18).

The phrase from Roman 9:23, "the riches of His glory," is deceptively simple. Anyone can understand that—or can he? Does it mean his "glorious riches?" as some think or the "riches [wealth] of His glory" (whatever that is)? It is hard to say, in and of itself. But use of the word *glory* elsewhere in Romans makes the second interpretation seem preferable.

In Romans 3:23, for example, Paul shows how, because of sin, both Jew and Greek have come short of "the glory of God." There it seems certain that *glory* stands on its own two feet as something attainable, that human beings have failed to attain. In Romans 5:2, those who are saved are said to look forward with hope (expectation) to the "glory of God." *Glory* is again set forth as a definable entity, not yet attained, but because of Christ, attainable by those who are saved. In Romans 8:18, Paul writes of "the glory to be revealed" in contrast to the sufferings of the present era. Once more, "glory" is largely in the future, but it is something coming to believers. And, of course, in Romans 9:23 he says the vases of mercy were prepared beforehand for glory. Glory is something given to them or that happens to them.

But what is this glory to which believers look forward and which unconverted sinners fall woefully short of attaining?

The word "glory" is used in the Scriptures in at least two senses. It may refer to

1. Reputation and fame, or to

2. The splendor of shining light.

In the first sense, both the Old and New Testament words for glory are brought together by the apostle Paul in II Corinthians 4:17, where he writes about the "weight of glory." The Old Testament term means "weighty, heavy." When someone is important, he is called heavy. When the importance of the part he plays in society is stressed, he is said to have weight. The use is much like our recent phrase, "Now that's heavy [important, overwhelming], man." In modern English we also say about someone who is powerful for some reason: "He's a heavyweight."

And we talk of giving something "its full weight." All of these expressions in English focus on some aspect of the Hebrew term for glory.

To "glorify" God, then, means to ascribe to Him the full weight of His place in anything. The New Testament word for glory means "fame," "good opinion." When one gives glory to another, he speaks good words about him; he spreads his fame abroad. Both usages coalesce in II Corinthians 4:17, where Paul speaks of the tremendous future of the believer. It is weighty and worth talking about!

The second use of the word refers to the brilliance and shining that accompanies God, the angels, and all that has to do with the heavens. Whenever the unseen world comes into contact with and is manifested to us in this world, it comes in a flood of light. When angels appeared to the shepherds at Christ's birth, "the glory of the Lord shown all around them." Moses' face glowed when he came away from meeting with God on the mountain. In the transfiguration of Christ the true splendor of His being burst forth, causing even His clothes to glitter and glisten.

To which of these two senses does Romans 9:22, 23 refer? To weighty fame or to outshining brilliance? Doubtless to the second. This is because the city is glorious, our bodies will be made like His glorious body, and the Lamb Himself is the Light and splendor of all that exists in the heavenly realm.

The place to which believers are going is so shining, so perfect, so splendid, so fresh and unsoiled, that Paul refers to it as "glory." What we will receive and where we are going are both called "glory," because the outstanding characteristic of all is its shining beauty.

The word "glory," though used elsewhere in other ways, then, here seems to be used to indicate all the wonder of the heavenly kingdom as it will be manifested at death and especially at the coming of Christ. The same thought appears elsewhere in the Bible. Christ's return to the Father is called an entrance into glory (Luke 24:26). In I Peter 5:10 the apostle writes of the eternal glory into which believers are called at death, as does Paul in I Thessalonians 2:12. This future glory, however, is beyond adequate human description. That is why Paul, pulling out all the stops, calls it "an eternal weight of glory *beyond all comparison*" (II Corinthians 4:17).

The Grand Demonstration will not be complete until all those whom God has redeemed are glorified with the splendor they will receive at judgment, and until all those who reject Christ are separated "from the presence of the Lord and from the glory of His might" (II Thessalonians 1:9).

Think of it—prostitutes, murderers, gossips, homosexuals, liars, adulterers, thieves and sinners of every description not only cleansed from their sins, but transformed in their habits, their attitudes, and their thoughts so that they have been "made perfect" (Hebrews 13:21)! But not only that. They will have been glorified so that they too "shine as the brightness of the firmament" (Daniel 12:3, Berkeley). The calling of elect sinners has as its object, says Paul, to "secure for yourselves the glory of our Lord Jesus Christ" (II Thessalonians 2:14). Truly, that *will* be a Grand Demonstration of mercy and grace.

But even now—to a very limited extent—God's attributes of mercy and grace are displayed to His glory (fame) and honor whenever a sinner is saved and his life begins to reflect (more and more, as he grows from "glory to glory") the glory of the Lord (II Corinthians 3:18).

Without a doubt, the glory to come is something about which every believer should be fully informed. The Scriptures say enough about it. Angels are aware of it and marvel. If we could but understand, even minimally, what future glorification means, we would not allow present troubles to overwhelm us. Rather, we would call even the most severe persecutions and afflictions "light" when compared with the eternal weight of glory that awaits us in heaven. What a Grand

Demonstration it will be when Jesus returns to be *glorified* by all His saints. It is one that will last forever, as men and angels and all the universe, observing for all eternity, will continually praise God for it.

11

DESTRUCTION, POWER, AND WRATH

What if God,
wishing to demonstrate His wrath
and to make known His power
endured with great patience
the vases of wrath fitted for destruction,
in order to make known
the riches of His glory
toward the vases of mercy,
that He designed beforehand for glory
(Romans 9:22, 23).

Destruction, *power*, and *wrath*—yes, those are the three words Paul uses in Roman 9:22, 23 to describe the fate of unrepentant sinners. What do these words mean, and exactly how are they used?

Destruction is the end result of almighty power released toward those against whom God's wrath has been building. The fundamental meaning of the word *destruction* is "ruin, loss or waste." By some, *destruction* has been wrongly interpreted to mean annihilation—non-existence. As a result, they see in the word the eventual wiping out of the wicked.

But that is not the meaning of either the Greek term or the English word by which it is translated. The English *to destroy* comes from the Latin words *struo*, "to build," and the negative prefix, *de*. The combination means, literally, "to unbuild," that is, "to undo." It has the idea of taking apart whatever was put together or undoing what was done. To destroy a fort is to leave it in ruins (not to annihilate it). To destroy a man financially is to leave him in financial ruin. It exactly approximates the Greek. To destroy a human being eternally is to leave him in spiritual ruins. His life, for eternity, will be in ruins. He will be a waste, a complete loss, spiritually.

All vain boasting will be smashed. Every plan will be shattered. Hope of ever recouping from the ruin will be gone. Desires and wishes will all be dashed to the ground. There will be no future to look forward to, and the present will be wrecked. All you can say is that the man is ruined. In some ways, this word is the most fearful description of the eternal destiny of the wicked. Think of it—to know that there will never again be any hope for anything! That is simply terrible to contemplate.

But what is it that will bring about this devastation? The second word makes that clear: God's own *power* released against sinners. A hurricane can wreck destruction upon a region, a tornado can rip up houses and reign death upon a city. Fire sweeping up canyons can burn communities to the ground; earthquakes can turn countries into rubble. Bombs, missiles and atomic weapons can release energy beyond comprehension. But these, or any other earthly manifestations of power, can't hold a candle to the power of God. His power is the source of all other power. All created power summed up together is not equal to it. We cannot begin to compare the power generated by a million suns to the power of God.

And it is this power—God's power—that will be unleashed against the vases of wrath fitted for destruction! The ruin left after the release of such power could not be more complete.

Why? Because destruction by God's power issues forth from His *wrath*. There are two words for wrath in the New Testament. One means a growing, passionate feeling of hostility pent up within; the other, this anger released in an outburst of power. It is the former term that Paul used in Romans 9 to describe the longsuffering of God during which His anger is coming to a boil. There are minor manifestations of that wrath now (cf. Romans 1:18), but at the second coming, the unsaved will experience the beginning of an unending stream of anger that will pour forth continually from the inner being of God for all eternity upon them. His justice and holiness will be satisfied. This wrath will be not only perpetual, but unrelenting. It will not slacken or abate. It will demonstrate to all concerned with the Grand Demonstration the holy hatred God has for sin.

Throughout all eternity, then, beings from all the universe, will see not only the display of God's incredible grace and will marvel and praise Him for it, but they will also stand in awe and holy fear as they view the eternal wrath of God streaming forth from the heavenly throne of justice.

12

CONCLUSION

In Him we were chosen
as His inheritance, being predestined
according to the purpose of the One
Who is operating everything
in agreement with the counsel of His will,
so that we may be
the praise of His glory . . .
(Ephesians 1:11-12a).

If you have continued with me this far, as we have been traveling through some very rough terrain, you know that I have attempted to contribute one thing in this book—a clear understanding of how the so-called problem of evil must be solved for the Christian. Evil exists in God's world because it serves the holy purpose of enabling God to demonstrate His grace and mercy as well as His power and wrath.

God cannot pour out wrath upon righteous beings; and righteous persons do not need salvation. Hence, evil. But it is wrath justly deserved, grace entirely undeserved.

There is no way to soften the impact of the teaching of the Scriptures for a humanistic mindset, whether it be in a pagan or in a Christian who has been brainwashed by psychological and philosophical thought. Man-centered thinking prefers, as the greatest good in life, the self-actualization of human beings to the self-actualization of God. And its devotees cry out loudly against anyone else who does. To accept the teaching of Romans 9 requires a radical reorientation of one's perspective on the ways of God and man.

If you are still perplexed, finding it difficult to accept what I have written, but unable to explain away the obvious import of Romans 9, your perplexity has a base. The thrust of this book runs counter to almost everything you have ever heard, not only outside, but also inside of the church. I know that. While you should not exchange your beliefs too easily, and only for those you think are more biblical, neither should you lightly dismiss those who differ if they offer scriptural reasons for what they say. Your obligation is to search the Scriptures daily to see if these things be so.

If you allow the full force of the truth, that in this world God is demonstrating His nature to all the universe, to filter down into your heart, soon, like the young FBI employee, you too will discover your outlook on history, on your personal affairs, and on God Himself greatly expanded.

Take the time to read and reread if necessary. After all, though I have tried to write so that almost any Christian may read and understand, rather than writing for theologians, in this book we have been considering some of the most profound issues possible. Take plenty of time, all you need, to think these things through.

And now, may the all-knowing, all-powerful God of creation bless you with all spiritual knowledge so that you may truly see and fully appreciate the Grand Demonstration of His character!

OTHER BOOKS FROM EASTGATE

PsychoHeresy: The Psychological Seduction of Christianity by Martin and Deidre Bobgan exposes the fallacies and failures of psychological counseling theories and therapies for one purpose: to call the church back to curing souls by means of the Word of God and the work of the Holy Spirit rather than by man-made means and opinions. Besides revealing the anti-Christian biases, internal contradictions, and documented failures of secular psychotherapy, *PsychoHeresy* examines various amalgamations of secular psychologies with Christianity and explodes firmly entrenched myths that undergird those unholy unions.

12 Steps to Destruction: Codependency/Recovery Heresies by Martin and Deidre Bobgan provides essential information for Christians about codependency/recovery teachings, Alcoholics Anonymous, Twelve-Step groups, and addiction treatment programs. They are examined from a biblical, historical, and research perspective. The book urges believers to trust in the sufficiency of Christ and the Word of God instead of the Twelve Steps and codependency/recovery theories and therapies.

Lord of the Dance: The Beauty of the Disciplined Life by Deidre Bobgan is for women who desire a deeper, more meaningful, intimate walk with the Savior. From her background in classical ballet, Deidre draws unique parallels between the training of a ballet dancer and a disciplined, graceful walk with God.